Napoleon

Lucy Lethbridge

Illustrated by Robin Lawrie

History consultant: Dr. Michael Rowe
King's College, London

Reading consultant: Alison Kelly
Roehampton University

Series editor: Lesley Sims

Designed by Russell Punter

First published in 2005 by Usborne Publishing Ltd.,
Usborne House, 83-85 Saffron Hill, London
EC1N 8RT, England.
www.usborne.com

Printed in China. UE.
First published in America in 2005.

Contents

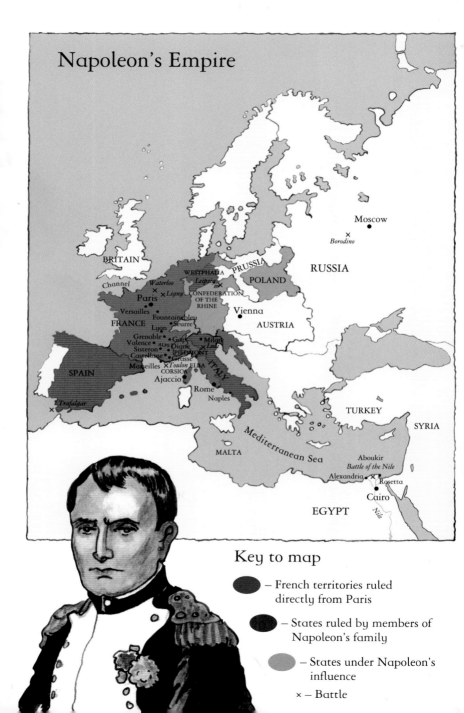

Napoleon's Empire

BRITAIN
Channel
Moscow
× *Borodino*
WESTPHALIA
× *Waterloo* *Leipzig*
PRUSSIA
POLAND
RUSSIA
Paris × *Ligny*
CONFEDERATION
OF THE
RHINE
Versailles
Vienna
FRANCE
Fountainebleu
AUSTRIA
Lyon × Seurre
Grenoble • Gap × Milan
Valence • Digne × *Lodi*
ALPS PIEDMONT
Sisteron •
Castellane • Grasse
Marseilles × *Toulon* ELBA
ITALY
CORSICA
SPAIN
Ajaccio •
Rome
Naples
TURKEY
SYRIA
× *Trafalgar*
Mediterranean Sea
MALTA
Aboukir
Battle of the Nile
Alexandria × Rosetta
Cairo
EGYPT
Nile

Key to map

● – French territories ruled
directly from Paris

● – States ruled by members of
Napoleon's family

● – States under Napoleon's
influence

× – Battle

Chapter 1

A family of rebels

Even before he was born, Napoleon was thrust into war. When his mother Letizia was pregnant with him, she was swept up in a fight for Corsica, her island home. The island had been taken over by the French, and furious islanders – including Napoleon's father Carlo – banded together to make lightning attacks on French soldiers.

Carlo Bonaparte, a member of one of Corsica's most noble families, fled into the hills with Letizia, and Joseph, their baby son.

The family camped out in a granite cave, high up in the mountains. It was the perfect vantage point to spy on French ships, although bullets whistled past them whenever they left the cave.

The rebel Corsicans fought hard, but they were no match for a French army of 22,000 soldiers. Outnumbered, they were forced to surrender. Reluctantly, Carlo had to return to the Corsican capital, Ajaccio, where he found a job as a lawyer.

The French raised their flag triumphantly over the city and announced that from then on the island's official language would be French.

Carlo hated to see the French in power but he couldn't bear to leave his island. Besides, Letizia was nearing the end of her pregnancy – and the end came sooner than anyone expected. One hot August day in 1769, she had to race home from church, arriving back just before a weak and feeble Napoleon was born.

Despite being premature, Napoleon grew up strong and healthy, if small for his age. He was stubborn, lively and curious about everything. When he was only eight, he took a pony and

went off to the local mill, to find out exactly how much corn it ground in an hour.

He also played endless games with his brother Joseph. The two could not have been more different. Joseph was as quiet as Napoleon was boisterous, though he could often be provoked to violent wrestling matches. In the end, Letizia had to clear a room full of furniture for them.

Whatever Napoleon did, he grew so absorbed, he'd forget the time.

"Napoleon!" Letizia would call from the house. "Lunch is ready."

But he wasn't interested in food —
except for the fat black cherries from
the tree hanging over their garden
wall. Napoleon could eat those until
he felt sick.

Every summer, the family headed
to the mountains to escape the
unbearable heat. Taking mattresses,
they slept on the floor of a farmhouse,
surrounded by herds of goats and fields
of olive and lemon trees. Napoleon
would stay up late, thrilled by his
cousins' stories about a ghostly boy
who beat his drum
on stormy nights.

When Napoleon was six, Letizia
had a third son, Lucien, followed two
years later by a daughter named
Maria Anna. By now, their father
Carlo had become such a famous figure
that the French invited him to be a
member of the Corsican government.
He strode about town dressed in a
curled wig, silk stockings and big-
buckled shoes, earning
himself the nickname
Bonaparte the
Magnificent.

Carlo was even
invited to France
where he met the
French king,
Louis XVI, and
his wife, Marie
Antoinette.

Although the Bonapartes were powerful in Corsica and led a fairly comfortable life, they weren't rich. So it was a great relief for Letizia and Carlo when the French Governor of Corsica — who had become a close friend — offered to send the oldest boys to private schools in France. Joseph, his parents decided, should train for the church; Napoleon would enter the army.

Napoleon was barely nine years old when he was sent away from home to a military academy in France. Even though she was sure she was doing the right thing, Letizia couldn't help feeling sorry for her son — a small, nervous figure on the quayside. As he waited to board his ship to Marseilles, she bent to kiss him goodbye.

"Be brave, Napoleon," she whispered.

Chapter 2

The young soldier

Despite their young age, the academy was strict and worked the pupils hard. Woken at six every morning, the boys were kept busy until 'lights out' at ten. Napoleon slept on a hard iron bed, in a dormitory with ten other cadets. Each boy had a jug of water and a bowl to wash in. In the winter it was so cold the water froze in the jugs. The only peace was found in the garden, where each cadet had some land to grow fruit and vegetables.

At first, Napoleon was utterly miserable. He missed his home, the other cadets teased him because he was so small and everyone laughed at his French, in its thick Corsican accent. But Napoleon turned on the boys furiously, lashing out with his fists. After a few bloody noses, the jeers turned to respect.

To take his mind off home, Napoleon buried himself in lessons. He loved mathematics and geography and he adored fencing, his blade a blur as he fought.

After some months at the academy, Napoleon decided he wanted to join the navy and rigged up a hammock in his dormitory. But by his teens, he was set c   g ldier. At just 1   ted from the   chool in Paris and became a second lieutenant in the French Army.

In all this time, Napoleon had not been home to Corsica, where his mother had produced four more children. Then, during Napoleon's year in Paris, the family was shattered when Carlo died of cancer. Suddenly, Letizia was a widow with a huge family to support and Napoleon felt responsible for looking after them all.

Promising to help out, he was sent
on his first posting, to an army
barracks in the town of Valence. This
was fairly near Marseilles, where boats
sailed for   ica. Within   ou
years, Napo   n's brother
come to live w th him. By
L izia was poverty-stricken, but
Napoleon saved whenever he
could, sending her money
from his pay each week.

Most of his days were spent
on guard duty or on parade,
marching men up and
down. They were so far
from any cities, there
was little else
to do.

In his spare time, Napoleon devoured books, making notes on quirky facts that caught his imagination. But his life was lonely and uneventful... until he was ordered to the town of Seurre, northeast of Valence, with a hundred other soldiers.

"There's trouble," explained his Colonel. "The townspeople are rioting. They claim someone is stealing their wheat. Anyway, the town needs soldiers to keep order."

Napoleon arrived to see a large mob gathered by the river. People in the crowd were shouting and shaking their fists at a boat, which was filled with sacks bulging with wheat.

"We grew that!" shouted a man. "And we've been paid a pittance for it."

"What do you expect?" another asked

bitterly. "The rich want to keep us poor."

The crowd melted away as Napoleon arrived and the boat sailed off quickly. But Napoleon had seen the faces of the mob: pale, hollow-cheeked and hungry. He remembered his father's stories of the French king and queen and their magnificent court. Carlo had said the walls of the palace at Versailles were covered in real gold. The queen even had her own flock of sheep, just to play with. No wonder these people were angry, he thought. They had nothing.

A few months after the riot, Napoleon was reading in his room when a fellow officer burst in.

"Put your book down, Napoleon!" he cried. "I have incredible news. There's been a revolution. The people of Paris have attacked the city prison and they're demanding the king hand over his power to the people."

Chapter 3

Revolution!

At the age of 22, and already a colonel, Napoleon was in Paris seeing the chaos for himself. As he rode through the streets, he gazed in horror at the devastated city. Men and women in the red hats of revolutionaries were running everywhere, brandishing guns and pointed sticks.

"We want the king's heart to cook over a fire!" they yelled outside the palace, pelting the windows with stones.

Louis XVI appeared nervously at his window, only for people to boo and scream at him. When the king's guards tried to make the crowd disperse, angry revolutionaries broke through the palace gates and hacked down the guards with sticks and axes. Napoleon watched as pools of blood spread along the ground where the royal soldiers fell.

Soon, revolutionaries were swarming through the palace, carrying piles of the queen's clothes and shoes, and

throwing china, jewels and paintings out of the windows.

Napoleon agreed with them that everyone should be equal, but the thought of power had turned this mob crazy. It seemed they just wanted to kill the rich.

In the middle of the city, the mob set up a terrible machine, *la guillotine*. Its sharp blade sliced off the head of every noble the mob could find. Eventually, the guillotine chopped off the heads of the king and queen themselves. The crowd laughed and danced wildly, as they stuck the heads on poles and paraded them around Paris.

The king was quickly replaced by a group of Republicans, who wanted France to be a Republic where the people governed themselves. Led by a bloodthirsty revolutionary, Robespierre, they began a reign of terror. Taking charge of the army, they ordered it to put down all uprisings. Then, in the seaside town of Toulon, the Republicans faced their most serious threat.

Toulon had been surrounded by armies from Britain and Spain, who planned to attack the Republic and put Louis XVI's son on the throne. British and Spanish ships waited in the port and their soldiers were stationed in forts on all the hills around the town. It looked impossible to get past them, but that didn't deter Napoleon.

He led 2,000 soldiers straight up to

the city walls. The sky was dark with storm clouds, and bullets flew at them through heavy rain. Amidst terrified shouts, Napoleon urged his men on. Toulon was his first real battle and his first taste of victory. Napoleon's rise to power had begun.

Less than a year later, his world was turned upside down when Robespierre was executed and Napoleon was thrown in jail. His career might have ended there, but the new French government, known as the Directors, quickly realized he was too valuable a commander to leave rotting in prison.

He was brought back to Paris as a general where he helped the Directors quash the last minor revolts in the city.

"Give them a whiff of gunshot," he told soldiers facing the angry crowds.

His next step was to find a wife. Napoleon liked petite, softly-spoken women and Josephine de Beauharnais seemed perfect. She was also clever, witty, light-hearted – and six years older. Always elegantly dressed, she loved clothes and her brown hair curled fashionably over her forehead.

Josephine had been married before, to a French nobleman, and she had a son and daughter. But her husband had been guillotined during the revolution and she had been locked up in prison. Now, she and her children were living in a small house in Paris.

Napoleon fell almost instantly in love. His mother disapproved of Josephine, warning him that she had expensive tastes. But Napoleon was determined to marry her. She was his ideal wife. They were married the year they met, in the newly-established marriage registry in Paris.

Two days after the wedding, Napoleon went to war again, this time in Italy. Emperor Francis of Austria, a nephew of Marie Antoinette's, had joined forces with King Victor of Piedmont, a small kingdom to the north of Italy. Together, they intended to avenge the deaths of Louis XVI and Marie Antoinette.

Napoleon was sent to take command of the French army in Italy, but before he could plan a strategy, he had to sort out the army. He was appalled to find the men had little training and less equipment. Many soldiers didn't even have proper boots, but marched for miles with strips of cloth tied around their feet. Napoleon's first move was to order huge supplies of meat, bread and boots for everyone.

Though heavily outnumbered, the French troops were quick. They were also determined to do their best for the "Little Corporal" – their nickname for Napoleon. Soon, they were winning victory after victory. They thought they were unstoppable... until they came to Lodi, just south of Milan.

Thousands of Austrian soldiers were waiting on the other side of a river, their guns aimed directly at them. Napoleon saw it was time to take a risk. He decided to storm the wooden bridge across the river, leading his men into the oncoming Austrian troops under a hail of gunfire.

His strategy worked. As the French soldiers swarmed over the bridge, the Austrians turned and fled. After the Battle of Lodi, Napoleon jubilantly raised the French flag over the palace in Milan.

"What I have done so far is a mere nothing!" he declared.

More battles followed, as Napoleon and his army triumphantly headed south. When they entered Rome and faced the Pope, Pius VI – who hated the new French Republic – they emptied his chests of gold. Next they marched on Vienna, the capital of Austria, where Emperor Francis had no choice but to make peace.

Chapter 4

Capturing Egypt

The French were bursting with pride and few were happier than the soldiers. As the Directors couldn't pay them, Napoleon took money from the conquered states. But he missed his wife. Every day, he sent long, loving letters, begging her to join him. Eventually, he threatened to leave and the Directors hastily sent Josephine to meet him.

"He worships me so much," she told a friend. "I think he will go crazy."

Napoleon returned to Paris a hero and the Directors urged him to turn his attention to Britain.

"It's a terrible idea," thought Napoleon. "Their navy is too strong. We'll never win a fight in the Channel."

Instead, he and the Foreign Minister, Charles Talleyrand, suggested going to Egypt, to block Britain's trade route to India. Eager to explore Egypt too, Napoleon asked scientists, historians and artists to join his army. Egypt was ruled by the Mamelukes, who were famous for being fierce fighters, but Napoleon was sure he could beat them.

He set off with a massive fleet of 180 ships, carrying 700 horses, 1,000 guns, and 17,000 men. The ships arrived first at the tiny island of Malta, which they captured without firing a single shot.

In Egypt, Napoleon marched on Alexandria, the second largest city, quickly taking it from the poorly prepared Mamelukes. Then came a long march across the desert to Cairo.

It was the hottest time of year and the soldiers struggled on under a blistering sun. They were constantly thirsty and bitten by millions of flies.

Even so, Napoleon won another swift victory. In Cairo, he established a French colony and set up the "Institute of Egypt" in an abandoned palace, to study the country. Before long, the Institute was printing newspapers to give a French slant on Egyptian affairs. And, all the time, Napoleon was disciplining and training his troops.

Meanwhile, the experts who had accompanied Napoleon were eagerly studying the mummies and ancient monuments they found half-buried in desert sand. Many relics were covered in strange carvings, or hieroglyphs, which baffled everyone. Then a French soldier made what was to be a crucial discovery. In the port of Rosetta, he found an ancient, black stone inscribed with three languages. A quarter of a century later, when scholars translated the they unlocked the of the hieroglyph world of Ancient Egypt.

Napoleon was fascinated by Egypt, but his stay was rudely interrupted when British ships, under the command of Admiral Nelson, slipped around the headland of the coastal town of Aboukir. Launching a surprise attack, Nelson blasted French ships moored along the Nile, smashing them to smithereens. The Battle of the Nile was a major victory for the British. Even

worse, it encouraged Turkey to declare war on France. Napoleon immediately led his army into Syria, although he came up against the British again and was forced to retreat back to Egypt.

He was fighting a Turkish invasion when news came from France that the country was in chaos. There were even reports that Louis XVI's brother was going to be put on the throne. Napoleon abandoned his army and raced home.

He was lucky to get there alive. As he crossed the Mediterranean, his ship was constantly dodging the British, who were out for his blood. And back in France, Napoleon found the country was almost bankrupt. Workers didn't have jobs and it was unsafe to go anywhere, because so many desperate men had become bandits. Something had to be done. Disgruntled politicians and army officers started meeting secretly in Napoleon's house in Paris, to plan overthrowing the government.

On November 10th, 1799, Napoleon strode into the French parliament, followed by a few soldiers with loaded guns and bayonets. The politicians were outraged. "Armed men in parliament?" they shouted. "Dictator! Outlaw!"

Some rushed forward to confront Napoleon, who was pushed and shoved. Protected by his soldiers, Napoleon quickly left. But his brother Lucien, who had seen everything, accused the men of trying to kill Napoleon. This enraged the rest of Napoleon's soldiers, waiting outside. They stormed the chamber and the politicians fled, diving through windows to escape. Napoleon had won.

Napoleon saw that the French people needed to know their government was acting for them. Ideally, they would have a written statement, laying down the structure of the government and saying what it could and couldn't do.

"What France needs," he thought, "is a constitution!" He drafted it in just a month and headed the new government himself, taking the title First Consul. He was still only 30 years old. But he was also battle-worn and, with a new, cropped haircut, he looked older. He was a short man, only 1.58m tall (just over 5ft), but people who met him were most struck by his eyes, which would hold them in a piercing gaze.

As First Consul, Napoleon

lived in richly furnished rooms at the Tuileries Palace, which had once belonged to Louis XVI.

Unlike the ex-king, Napoleon had simple tastes. When not in official dress, he wore plain clothes, with no decoration except a tiny "tricolor" rosette – the emblem of the new France – in his hat. He hated fussy food, preferring lentils, potatoes and, occasionally, chicken. His only indulgences were long, hot baths and snuff, which he kept in a small box in his pocket.

Josephine was his opposite. Extremely extravagant, she adored fine clothes. In one year alone, she bought 528 pairs of shoes and 38 hats trimmed with heron feathers. The entire country gossiped about the vast sums she spent and her debts annoyed Napoleon, although he liked seeing her dressed up.

Wanting to please her, he bought a house called Malmaison, where she planted a wonderful rose garden. His one regret was that they had no children. Napoleon began to wonder if he should divorce Josephine and find a wife who might bear him a son.

Chapter 5

Coronation

One evening, Napoleon and Josephine went for an evening drive in their carriage. As they turned into a narrow street, a horse and cart swerved in front of them. The carriage driver whipped up the horses and tried to overtake the cart. Suddenly, there was a huge explosion. It lit up the sky with fireworks and flung Napoleon and Josephine across the carriage with a bang.

The cart driver had set off a homemade bomb, which tore through the streets and houses, killing nine people and injuring many more. The one person he wanted dead – Napoleon – was shaken but unhurt. It was one of many plots against him, mostly from allies of the old French royal family who were backed by Britain.

Napoleon realized he had to make his position more secure. In that way, he thought, he would make France safer. The people had had a royal family for more than a thousand years. Perhaps they were not ready to give up the monarchy completely.

He decided that the answer was to be crowned emperor of the French. He would hold a magnificent coronation ceremony with crowns, thrones and fur and velvet robes. This would unite everyone in support of Napoleon and the new France.

Napoleon chose an eagle and bees for his emblem and designed himself a crown shaped like the laurel wreaths worn by Roman emperors. He was making all the ancient traditions of a royal family from scratch.

On the day of the coronation,
Napoleon dressed in silk, topped by
a long velvet cloak lined with ermine
and embroidered with gold bees. The
Pope himself was summoned from
Rome to attend, though he simply
watched as Napoleon took charge,
crowning himself.

The new emperor wasted no time in expanding his empire. Soon, it covered over half of Europe and Napoleon was interested in every detail of running it. One of his changes was to introduce a simpler system of law, the *Code Napoléon*, which gave everyone equal rights. Even so, he didn't think ordinary people should rule themselves. Instead, he thought, they needed one all-powerful but wise ruler: him.

As he took over more of Europe, he replaced the old royal families with his own. He made his eldest brother Joseph King of Spain and another, Jerome, King of Westphalia. But he still fretted that he had no son to inherit his empire.

"I will have to marry again," he realized. So, though they remained friends, he and Josephine divorced.

Napoleon cast around for a likely candidate for his new empress and picked out Marie Louise, daughter of Francis, the emperor of Austria. She was pretty and, at just 18, over twenty years younger than Napoleon. A year after their marriage she gave birth to his son. The delighted emperor immediately made him King of Rome.

But Britain was still his enemy and the Royal Navy, led by Admiral Nelson, scored a spectacular victory over the French at the Battle of Trafalgar. And another enemy was waiting in the wings: Russia.

Alexander I of Russia had decided Napoleon was becoming too powerful. Having veered between supporting France and Britain for several years, Alexander began to back Britain again. Napoleon was furious and led a Grand Army of over 600,000 soldiers into Poland. He was ready for a major battle – the sort he always won outright – but Alexander simply retreated every time Napoleon's army drew near.

At the village of Borodino they fought at last, a long and bloody battle that left thousands dead on both sides. This wasn't the triumph Napoleon had hoped for but, gathering his remaining forces, he marched on Moscow.

It was autumn when they arrived, and already growing colder. Napoleon waited for Tsar Alexander to declare peace. He waited in vain. Alexander refused to talk of peace and Napoleon did not want to stay in Moscow. He knew about Russia's freezing winters and wanted to get home to the comfort of Paris. So he made the fateful decision to leave. By now, it was October and winter was setting in.

Napoleon's army left Moscow in a long train of horses, wagons and cannons. There was enough food for the men for 20 days but only enough horse feed for a week and, with the frost hardening, there would be no grass. After three weeks of walking, the wind was bitterly cold and the horses were reduced to eating the bark of pine trees.

The nearest large town was 200 miles away. Sometimes, the desperate soldiers approached Russian villagers for food and shelter – and had their throats slit. At night, the men huddled against the bodies of dying horses for warmth.

At long last, the army arrived in Poland. Thousands had died on the way and the emperor himself was nearly unconscious from the cold. The long, terrible march across Russia had taken nearly seven weeks.

Chapter 6

Exile

Napoleon's army was destroyed and the Russians marched on Europe. As Napoleon desperately raised a new army, Alexander joined forces with the Prussian king and Austrian emperor. At the Battle of Leipzig, Napoleon's troops were wiped out by almost half a million enemy soldiers. After that, Napoleon's empire crumbled fast. His brother Jerome had to give back his throne in Westphalia and, as if things weren't bad enough, the British began to advance on his brother Joseph in Spain.

Soon, a great army of France's enemies were marching on Paris. Napoleon and his family took flight in their coronation coach. The emperor tried to rally the people to his side, but they had become frightened. When the Russians, Austrians and Prussians entered Paris, they encountered virtually no resistance.

51

Napoleon, Marie Louise and their son were in their palace at Fountainebleu, when they heard that France had fallen. Immediately, Napoleon took up his pen and signed a statement of abdication, giving up the throne.

Napoleon was exiled to the island of Elba, just off the coast of Italy. He was allowed to keep the title emperor, but now his entire empire was a tiny island only 29km (18 miles) long. He hoped that his wife and child might join him, but that was refused. As the emperor was escorted from the palace, many of his guards wept.

Elba is so small, few people had heard of it before Napoleon went there. But the Elbans had heard of Napoleon. When he disembarked from his ship, they gave him a rousing welcome.

It was typical of Napoleon that the next day he rode off at four in the morning to inspect his new home. The island was very poor and covered with dark chestnut forests. But Napoleon saw that, with firm leadership, the islanders could have a better life. In his first weeks, he set to work on a project to make the island self-sufficient. He encouraged the islanders to grow cauliflowers, lettuces and potatoes, and organized a waste collection in the small capital, Portoferraio. He had the streets paved and benches put on the quay. Then he decorated his house, with the drawing room painted with scenes from ancient Egypt.

He still hoped that Marie Louise would join him, but she returned to her father. Napoleon never heard from her again. Instead, his mother and sister Pauline came to live with him and they spent the evenings sitting in the garden or playing cards.

As the months went on, he began to receive visitors who told him the news of France. The French people missed Napoleon, who had been replaced by Louis XVI's brother, a king no one liked. In fact, they said, everyone was hoping that Napoleon might come back.

His supporters wore striped sashes and watch-chains to signal their loyalty and their numbers were growing. Napoleon, who could never sit still, began making plans.

British ships were guarding Elba, so he told his supporters to paint a large ship to look like a British one. Then he took six smaller ships, stocked them with food and provisions, and collected together all the men who were loyal to him.

His mother worried she would never see him again. "I suppose you must carry out your destiny," she sighed. But his sister Pauline urged him on.

"Better to die fighting than lazing your days away doing nothing!"

Luck was on his side. Napoleon boarded his disguised ship and slipped out of the port, unnoticed. He had just 1,000 men with him to fight the whole French army. Landing near Cannes, he began the march to Paris. First, he headed north to Grasse and then Castellane, crossing the Alps between Digne and Sisteron. He wound his way on, through Gap to Grenoble, then Lyon and Fontainebleau. Everywhere he went, people rushed out to cheer him on.

In Paris, Louis XVIII had already heard that Napoleon was on his way. He packed his bags, jumped into a carriage and rattled away from the city as fast as he could. When Napoleon entered Paris, he found streets lined with people throwing their hats in the air and shouting, "Long live the emperor!"

Napoleon returned to the Tuileries Palace and found his old rooms untouched. The rich furnishings and gold furniture were as he had left them. The emperor was back.

Not everyone was pleased to hear of Napoleon's return. In Vienna, foreign ministers from Britain, Prussia, Russia and Austria met to discuss what to do with this upstart who had escaped his island prison. Britain had troops near

Brussels and Britain's most famous general, the Duke of Wellington, declared he would fight Napoleon to the death if he dared to attack them.

"We'll give you every help," the Prussian leader assured him. "We have our own armies stationed nearby."

Napoleon prepared to attack. He was determined there would be no threat to him now that he was emperor of the French again and rode at the head of a mighty army.

"The French army is the finest in the world," he declared proudly, looking at the soldiers marching behind him.

When they reached the village of Ligny, they attacked the Prussians and defeated them easily. Then they pressed deeper into the countryside.

The Duke of Wellington, on the top of a high hill and seated on his horse Copenhagen, watched them through a spyglass. Below him stretched a plain known as the Field of Waterloo and thousands of French soldiers were setting up camp upon it.

As Napoleon attacked – uphill – the British formed themselves into squares, holding their muskets out in front of them. They fired desperately into the oncoming rush of French cavalry, who were waving terrifying curved sabres. The British soldiers knew their only chance was to stay together in their squares.

On and on the French horses came, pounding the mud with their hooves. The air was thick with gunpowder and smoke. Over the sound of clashing steel and gunfire rose the dreadful cries of wounded men and horses.

The battle raged for hours. Then suddenly, a trumpet sounded over the hill. It was the Prussians! They had gathered up their forces and come to join the battle.

The British swept down the hill in a great wave and the French knew it was all over. Their army scattered like startled sheep.

Napoleon, too, knew that he had finally been defeated. He scrambled into his carriage to flee, but the road was jammed by crowds of soldiers. So he leaped onto his horse and galloped across the fields to the coast.

When the British found his carriage, it was empty except for some rich furnishings and curtains. There was also a large container stowed under the seat — the emperor's solid-silver, portable toilet.

Napoleon didn't get far. When he reached the sea, he was picked up by a British ship and shut up in the hold. He had been emperor again for just 136 days.

This time, he was exiled to the island of St. Helena in the South Atlantic. Here, he was given a house and an Englishman, Hudson Lowe, to watch him. To Lowe's fury, Napoleon ordered him about as if he were still an emperor. Napoleon had servants, books, even a piano, but he had no freedom. While he could walk around the island as he pleased, he knew he would never be able to leave.

Napoleon was on the island for nearly six boring, miserable years, before he grew ill with stomach pains. He died on May 5 1821, at the age of 51, and was buried in a silk-lined coffin in a quiet spot on St. Helena. Years later, his body was taken to Paris and reburied. It is still there, in a magnificent tomb fit for an emperor.

Aug 1769 - I am born in Ajaccio, Corsica.

1778 - I'm sent to boarding school, where I learn to fight with my fists as well as swords.

1785 - I become a second lieutenant.

1793 - Louis XVI is executed. I recapture Toulon from the British and Spanish, impressing Robespierre. I am briefly imprisoned after Robespierre's execution, but later released.

1796 - I marry Josephine and take the army into Italy.

1798 - I conquer Egypt. Nelson takes me by surprise to win the Battle of the Nile.

1799 - I overthrow the Directors, before drafting France's Constitution and becoming First Consul.

1804 - I crown myself Emperor. (No one else is important enough.) I start expanding my Empire throughout Europe.

1805 - The British defeat me at the Battle of Trafalgar.

1810 - Hoping for an heir, I divorce Josephine and marry Marie Louise.

1811 - My son, the King of Rome, is born!

1812 - A disastrous campaign in Russia. I am defeated by the winter.

1813 - The Austrians, Russians and Prussians gang up against me.

1814 - I abdicate and am exiled on Elba but the French people want me back.

1815 - My triumphant return to France and the terrible Battle of Waterloo. This time I am exiled to St. Helena from where there is no chance of return.

May 5, 1821 - Napoleon dies of stomach cancer.